Cocktail
HOUR

Cocktail
HOUR

A MIXER OF QUIPS
AND QUOTATIONS

JESS BRALLIER and
SALLY CHABERT

OPEN ROAD

INTEGRATED MEDIA

NEW YORK

Copyright © 1996 by Jess M. Brallier and Sally Chabert

ISBN: 978-1-5040-9039-1

This edition published in 2024 by Open Road Integrated Media, Inc.
180 Maiden Lane
New York, NY 10038
www.openroadmedia.com

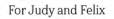

For Judy and Felix

INTRODUCTION

A good quotation is a wonderful thing. It is quickly accessible and easily consumed. It may inspire, amuse, or enlighten. Or better yet, it may do all three.

Quotes gathered on paper, then bound (a book!), are so special that there are, in print and available, more than five hundred themed collections of quotations, from those for women, lawyers, and middle managers, to those for cooks, gardeners, and lovers.

We compiled three of those published collections: *Lawyers and Other Reptiles*, *Medical Wit and Wisdom*, and *Presidential Wit and Wisdom*. In our research (which involves a tedious and primitive process of too many note cards) we often discover "rejected favorites"—quotes we admire but cannot use for the specific task at hand. We toss these cards into a box brought home from the local liquor store. Whenever friends visit, and after Twister wears thin, we turn to the "rejected favorites" box.

Recently it dawned upon us that there must be something very special about those quotes. We decided to study them. We dumped the box's cards onto the living room floor and dove in. Only minutes were required, for it was quickly apparent that the best of them were about drinking. We had, without purpose or vision, compiled within that old liquor box a refreshing little collection we've named *Cocktail Hour*.

As is true of any notion that suddenly strikes with great clarity, a collection of drinking quotes is *obvious*. After all, the very beauty of a quotation is the simplicity and clarity—and often wit—with which it comments on life. Let's consider a few observations:

Liquor loosens the tongue. The rate of commentary which is likely to produce a decent quotation drastically accelerates with drink, thus creating a virtual gold mine of quotes.

A good quote is far more likely to come out of the mouth of those people practiced in the economy of language. People such as writers, most of whom are drinkers!

Quotes are most memorable and insightful when they speak of life's extremes. Celebrating a victory? Marriage? Birth? Graduation? Fortune?

Well, then have a drink. Yet what of the other extreme? Darkness. Desolation. Dumpsters and gutters. Utter failure. What is the surest, most direct course to that edge, the one that borders on death, and—too often—crosses over? Drink, of course.

It is no wonder then that drinkers observe life—at its very best and its horrible worst—with such uniqueness. Thus, this collection.

And it's about time. The cocktail hour is back. After decades of extreme political correctness and legislated control of our personal vices and private time, the world remains imperfect. At moments, we need the calm influence, not the activist. In the 1990s, we've at last matured into adults, no longer mindless pawns within some overly-funded sociological experiment. So find the moment and enjoy it. Darken the room, play some jazz, share a stranger's smile, and sip a well-chilled martini.

But, some may ask, what does such a collection of quotes reveal about its compilers and its readers? Permit us to respond, appropriately enough, with a quote, in this case, one from a congressman responding to a constituent's query, "Where do you stand on whiskey?"

If, when you say whiskey you mean the Devil's brew, the poison scourge, the bloody monster that defiles innocence, dethrones reason, destroys the home, creates misery and poverty . . . takes the bread from the mouths of little children; if you mean the evil drink that topples the Christian man and woman from the pinnacles of righteous, gracious living into the bottomless pit of degradation and despair, shame and helplessness and hopelessness, then certainly I am against it with all of my power.

But, if, when you say whiskey, you mean the oil of conversation, the philosophic wine, the ale that is consumed when good fellows get together, that puts a song in their hearts and laughter on their lips, and the warm glow of contentment in their eyes; if you mean Christmas cheer; if you mean the stimulating drink that puts the spring in the old gentleman's step on a frosty morning; if you mean the drink that enables a man to magnify his joy and his happiness and to forget, if only for a little while, life's great tragedies, and the heartbreaks and sorrows; if you

mean that drink . . . then certainly I am
in favor of it.

—*Unknown**

And so it is in this same spirit that we bring you
Cocktail Hour.

Cheers!

* According to *Respectfully Quoted: A Dictionary of Quotations Requested from the Congressional Research Service* (Library of Congress), the author of this letter remains unknown. Former Representative D. R. Billy Matthews claims this story was told in the early 1960s by another member of Congress, who did not know the original author.

Cocktail
HOUR

The pause between the errors and trials of the day and the hopes of the night.

—*Herbert Hoover, on the cocktail hour*

I think a man ought to get drunk at least twice a year just on principle, so he won't let himself get snotty about it.

—*Raymond Chandler*

Alcohol is a very necessary article. It enables Parliament to do things at eleven at night that no sane person would do at eleven in the morning.

—*George Bernard Shaw*

One reason I don't drink is that I want to know when I am having a good time.

—*Nancy Astor*

Well they was a lot of people in the U.S. that was in flavor of Prohibition and finely congress passed a law making the country dry and the law went into effect about the 20 of Jan. 1920 and the night before it went into effect everybody had a big party on acct. of it being the last chance to get boiled. As these wds. is written the party is just beginning to get good.

—*Ring Lardner, 1925*

I haven't touched a drop of alcohol since the invention of the funnel.

—Malachy McCourt

One more drink and I'll be under the host.

—Dorothy Parker

Give strong drink unto him that is ready to perish, and wine unto those that be of heavy hearts.

Let him drink, and forget his poverty, and remember his misery no more.

—Proverbs 31:4–7

My grandmother is over eighty and still doesn't need glasses. Drinks right out of the bottle.

—*Henny Youngman*

I usually need a can of beer to prime me.

—*Norman Mailer*

When everybody says you are drunk, go to sleep.

—*Italian proverb*

In the summer I drink Guinness, which requires no refrigeration and no cooking—Guinness is a great day-shortener. If you get out of bed first thing and drink a glass, then the day doesn't begin until about twelve-thirty, when you come to again, which is nice. I try to live in a perpetual snooze.

—*Quentin Crisp*

Brandy and water spoils two good things.

—*Charles Lamb*

Gin was his tonic.

—*Al Drooz, sportswriter, on Hack Wilson*

If you drink, don't drive. Don't even putt.

—*Dean Martin*

They drink with impunity, or anybody who invites them.

—*Artemus Ward*

Let's get out of these wet clothes and into a dry martini.

—*Robert Benchley (also attributed to Billy Wilder and Alexander Woollcott)*

I always wake up at the crack of ice.

—*Joe E. Lewis*

It's a naive domestic burgundy without any breeding, but I think you'll be amused by its presumption.

—*James Thurber*

After the White House, what is there to do but drink?

—*Franklin Pierce*

He died of cirrhosis of the liver. It costs money to die of cirrhosis of the liver.

—*P. G. Wodehouse, "Success Story"*

Some people have an automatic, internal clock that wakes them up at the right time every morning; I have an automatic, internal "ginometer."

—*Anthony Dias Blue*

Whisky drowns some troubles and floats a lot more.

—Robert C. Edwards

I don't drink, I don't like it. It makes me feel good.

—Oscar Levant

Champagne for my sham friends; real pain for my real friends.

—Francis Bacon

Actually, it only takes one drink to get me loaded. Trouble is, I can't remember if it's the thirteenth or fourteenth.

—*George Burns*

I have to think hard to name an interesting man who does not drink.

—*Richard Burton*

Alcohol is nicissary f'r a man so that now an' thin he can have a good opinon iv himsilf, ondisturbed be th' facts.

—*Finley Peter Dunne*

When I have one martini, I feel bigger, wiser, taller. When I have a second, I feel superlative. When I have more, there's no holding me.

—*William Faulkner*

Coming of a temperance family, drunkenness had always been for me a symbol of freedom.

—*Louis MacNeice*

'Twas a woman who drove me to drink, and I never had the courtesy to thank her for it.

—*W. C. Fields*

Come quickly, I am tasting stars!

—*Dom Pérignon (1638–1715), at the moment of his discovery of champagne*

Alcohol is the anesthesia by which we endure the operation of life.

—*George Bernard Shaw*

Before I start to write, I always treat myself to a nice dry martini. Just one, to give me the courage to get started. After that, I am on my own.

—*E. B. White*

A man is never drunk if he can lay on the floor without holding on.

—*Joe E. Lewis*

No animal ever invented anything so bad as drunkenness or so good as drink.

—*G. K. Chesterton*

Watch out when the auctioneer calls some nineteenth-century wine "a graceful old lady whose wrinkles are starting to show through layers of makeup." That means the wine is undrinkable, and some fool will spend $500 for it.

—*Robert Parker*

I have taken more out of alcohol than alcohol has taken out of me.

—*Winston Churchill*

Connoisseurs who like their martinis very dry suggest simply allowing a ray of sunlight to shine through a bottle of Noilly Prat before it hits the gin.

—*Luis Buñuel*

There is no bad beer: some kinds are better than others.

—*Tom Hoza*

There are two reasons for drinking: one is, when you are thirsty, to cure it; the other, when you are not thirsty, to prevent it.

—*Thomas Love Peacock*

Somebody left the cork out of my lunch.

—*W. C. Fields*

I've made it a rule never to drink by daylight and never to refuse a drink after dark.

—*H. L. Mencken*

I envy people who drink—at least they know what to blame everything on.

—*Oscar Levant*

Rum, n. Generically, fiery liquors that produce madness in total abstainers.

—*Ambrose Bierce,* The Devil's Dictionary

Champagne?

Oh! What big bubbles.

Yes. They had big grapes that year.
>   —*Eve Floogle (Binnie Barnes), Mr. Parker (Robert*
>   *Benchley), and Fred Floogle (Fred Allen),*
>   *in* It's in the Bag

I am a stylist, and the most beautiful sentence
I have ever heard is, "Have one on the house."
>   —*Wilson Mizner*

He's the kind of guy who would throw a beer party and then lock the bathroom door on you.

—*George Raveling, on Bobby Knight*

Sometimes too much to drink is barely enough.

—*Mark Twain*

Like a camel, I can go without a drink for seven days—and have on several horrible occasions.

—*Herb Caen*

Alcohol is like love: the first kiss is *magic*, the second is intimate, the third is routine. After that you just take the girl's clothes off.

—*Raymond Chandler*

Romance, like alcohol, should be enjoyed, but should not be allowed to become necessary.

—*Edgar Z. Friedenberg*

Work is the curse of the drinking classes.

—*Mike Romanoff*

Drunks are rarely amusing unless they know some good songs and lose a lot at poker.

—*Karyl Roosevelt*

Some American writers who have known each other for years have never met in the daytime or when both were sober.

—*James Thurber*

You can't drown yourself in drink. I've tried: you float.

—*John Barrymore*

The best thing about a cocktail party is being asked to it.

—*Gerald Nachman*

I never drank anything stronger than beer before I was twelve.

—W. C. Fields

Teetotaler, n. One who abstains from strong drink, sometimes totally, sometimes tolerably totally.

—Ambrose Bierce, The Devil's Dictionary

There is nothing for a case of nerves like a case of beer.

—Joan Goldstein

If you drink enough wine, it doesn't matter how bad it is.

—*Judy Aviles*

Beer is the national drink, and the Danish national weakness is another beer.

—*Clementine Paddleford*

Wouldn't it be terrible if I quoted some reliable statistics which prove that more people are driven insane through religious hysteria than by drinking alcohol?

—*W. C. Fields*

Wine, n. Fermented grape-juice known to the Women's Christian Union as "liquor," sometimes as "rum." Wine, madam, is God's next best gift to man.

—*Ambrose Bierce*, The Devil's Dictionary

I am a prohibitionist. What I propose to prohibit is the reckless use of water.

—*Bob Edwards*

Prohibition makes you want to cry into your beer, and denies you the beer to cry into.

—*Don Marquis*

A soft drink turneth away company.

—*Oliver Herford*

To one large turkey add one gallon of vermouth and a demijohn of Angostura bitters. Shake.

—*F. Scott Fitzgerald's recipe for turkey cocktail*

A man is a fool if he drinks before he reaches fifty, and a fool if he doesn't drink afterward.

—*Frank Lloyd Wright*

The secret to a long life is to stay busy, get plenty of exercise, and don't drink too much. Then again, don't drink too little.

—*Hermann Smith-Johannson*

Water, taken in moderation, cannot hurt anybody.

—*Mark Twain*

You must be careful about giving any drink whatsoever to a bore. A lit-up bore is the worst in the world.

—David Cecil

A real woman could stop you from drinking.

It would have to be a real big woman.

—Susan Johnson (Jill Eikenberry) and Arthur Bach
(Dudley Moore), in Arthur

An alcoholic is someone you don't like who drinks as much as you do.

—Dylan Thomas

Through booze I met two Chief Justices, 50 world champs, six Presidents and DiMaggio and Babe Ruth.

—*Toots Shor*

Other drugs tend to make you introspective, contemplative of your own navel, whereas alcohol tends to make you contemplate other people's navels.

—*Morris Chafetz*

A moral species of beverage.

—*Douglas Sector, on beer*

Beer is not a good cocktail-party drink, especially in a home where you don't know where the bathroom is.

—*Billy Carter*

There are more old drunkards than old doctors.

—*Ben Franklin*

During one of my trips through Afghanistan, we lost our corkscrew. Had to live on food and water for several days.

—*Cuthbert J. Twillie (W. C. Fields),*
in My Little Chickadee

Do not allow children to mix drinks. It is unseemly and they use too much vermouth.

—*Fran Lebowitz*

Man, being reasonable, must get drunk;
The best of life is but intoxication.

—*Lord Byron*

Eat everything, drink everything and don't worry about anything. It's always nice to have a shot just before breakfast.

—*Mrs. Galsomina Del Vecchio, at age 108*

The brewery is the best drug store.

—*Pittsburgh proverb*

Wine is the most healthful and most hygienic of beverages.

—*Louis Pasteur*

Drink a glass of wine after your soup, and you steal a ruble from the doctor.

—*Russian proverb*

If you drink like a fish, swim, don't drive.

—*bumper sticker*

I drink to make other people seem interesting.

—*George Jean Nathan*

Drunkenness is simply voluntary insanity.

—*Seneca (4 B.C.–A.D. 65)*

I was so drunk last night I fell down and missed the floor.

—*Dean Martin*

When I read about the evils of drinking, I gave up reading.

—*Henny Youngman*

I'd take a bromo, but I can't stand the noise.

—*Joe E. Lewis, hung-over*

After four martinis, my husband turns into a disgusting beast. And after the fifth, I pass out altogether.

—*anonymous*

Always carry a corkscrew and the wine shall provide itself.

—*Basil Bunting*

I've never been drunk, but often I've been overserved.

—*George Gobel*

It provokes the desire, but it takes away the performance.

—*Shakespeare*

Teetotallers lack the sympathy and generosity of men that drink.

—*W. H. Davies*

Show me a nation whose national beverage is beer, and I'll show you an advanced toilet technology.

—*Mark Hawkins*

Only Irish coffee provides in a single glass all four essential food groups—alcohol, caffeine, sugar, and fat.

—*Alex Levine*

I must point out that my rule of life prescribes as an absolutely sacred rite smoking cigars and also the drinking of alcohol before, after, and if need be during all meals and in the intervals between them.

—*Winston Churchill*

If you resolve to give up smoking, drinking, and loving, you don't actually live longer, it just seems longer.

—*Felix Aviles*

He neither drank, smoked, nor rode a bicycle. Living frugally, saving his money, he died early, surrounded by greedy relatives. It was a great lesson to me.

—*John Barrymore*

Lastly (and this is, perhaps, the golden rule), no woman should marry a teetotaller....

—*Robert Louis Stevenson*

Drink the first. Sip the second slowly. Skip the third.

—*Knute Rockne*

I had my bad days on the field, but I didn't take them home with me. I left them in a bar along the way.

—*Bob Lemon*

I see three baseballs, but I only swing at the middle one.

—*Paul Waner, on hitting well after a drinking spree*

Only when I'm drunk.

—*Ruben Oliveras, on being asked if he ever drank*

The Yankees should have been easy to stalk because, belonging to a high-class ball club, they drank martinis and left a trail of olives.

—*John Lardner, on the New York Yankees hiring*

detectives to tail some of its players

There is much less drinking now than there was before 1927, because I quit drinking on May 24, 1927.

—*Rabbit Maranville*

If your doctor warns that you have to watch your drinking, find a bar with a mirror.

—*John Mooney*

If a guy can't get drunk by midnight, he ain't trying.

—*Toots Shor, on the World War II midnight liquor curfew*

That's not true. I've switched to Minneapolis now.

—*Gump Worsley, hockey player, on allegations that he did all his training in St. Paul bars*

There are people who strictly deprive themselves of each and every eatable, drinkable and smokable which has in any way acquired a shady reputation. They pay this price for health. And health is all they get for it.

—*Mark Twain*

Never refuse wine. It is an odd but universally held opinion that anyone who doesn't drink must be an alcoholic.

—P. J. O'Rourke

I drink every known alcoholic drink and enjoy 'em all. I learned early in life how to handle alcohol and never had any trouble with it. The rules are simple as mud: first, never drink if you've got any work to do. Never. If I've got a job of work to do at ten o'clock at night I won't take a drink until that time. Secondly, never drink alone. That's the way to become a drunkard. And thirdly, even if you haven't got any work to do, never drink while the sun is shining. Wait until it's dark. By that time you're near enough to bed to recover quickly.

—H. L. Mencken

Every businessman over 50 should have a daily nap and nip—a short nap after lunch and a relaxing highball before dinner.

—Dr. Sara Murray Jordan, gastroenterologist

The more specific the name, the better the wine.

—Frank Schoonmaker

I am a vegetarian—but I hear vodka comes from a potato.

—*Barbara Whiteman (Bette Midler), in* Down and Out in Beverly Hills

First you take a drink, then the drink takes a drink, then the drink takes you.

—*F. Scott Fitzgerald*

Drinking makes such fools of people, and people are such fools to begin with that it's compounding a felony.

—*Robert Benchley*

A man's prose style is very responsive—even a glass of sherry shows in a sentence.

—*John Cheever*

Drinking makes you loquacious, as we all know, and if what you've got for company is a piece of paper, then you're going to talk to it. Just try to enunciate, and try to make sense.

—*Madison Smartt Bell, on writing and drinking*

I can't write without wine.

—*Tennessee Williams*

Cybill, *one* of us drunk is witty and charming and amusing. *Both* of us drunk is just pathetic.

—*Mary Ann (Christine Baranski), in "Cybill"*

The whole ethic, the whole belief system implied in the cocktail party is: You never know. Anything is possible. What the hell? Why not? What was your name again?

—*Glenn O'Brien*

I never drink while I'm working, but after a few glasses, I get ideas that would never have occurred to me dead sober.

—*Irwin Shaw*

At the third cup, wine drinks the man.

—Hokekyō Sho, *a Buddhist Sanskrit text*

Young men are apt to think themselves wise enough, as drunken men are to think themselves sober enough.

—*Lord Chesterfield*

The British are like their own beer: froth on top, dregs at bottom, the middle excellent.

—*Voltaire*

Lady Nancy Astor: Winston, you are drunk!

Winston Churchill: Indeed, Madam, and you are ugly—but tomorrow I'll be sober.

I only wish I knew what brand of whiskey he drinks. I'd send a barrel or so to some of my other generals.

> —*Abraham Lincoln, on being warned that*
> *Ulysses S. Grant was "a confirmed drunk"*

. . . to abstain from all intoxicating beverages excepting on the advice of a physician or in case of actual disease, also excepting wine at public dinners.

—*pledge of the Saratoga, New York-based Union Temperance Society, the nation's first temperance society*

Better sleep with a sober cannibal than a drunken Christian.

—*Herman Melville*

Inflation has gone up over a dollar a quart.

—*W. C. Fields*

The worst thing about some men is that when they are not drunk they are sober.

—*William Butler Yeats*

The less I behave like Whistler's mother the night before, the more I look like her the morning after.

—*Tallulah Bankhead*

I'd rather have a free bottle in front of me than a prefrontal lobotomy.

—*Tom Waits*

Beware of the man who does not drink.

—*proverb*

I hate to advocate drugs, alcohol, violence, or insanity to anyone, but they've always worked for me.

—*Hunter S. Thompson*

A productive drink is the bane of moralists.

—*The Reverend Edward D. Townsend*

I can't die until the government finds a safe place to bury my liver.

—*Phil Harris*

I don't drink because drinking affects your decision making.

You may be right, I can't decide.
>   —*Burt Johnson (Stephen Elliott) and Arthur Bach*
>   *(Dudley Moore), in* Arthur

I drink when there is an occasion, and sometimes when there is no occasion.
>   —*Miguel de Cervantes*

There must be some good in the cocktail party to account for its immense vogue among otherwise sane people.
>   —*Evelyn Waugh*

He was an ingenious man that first found out eating and drinking.

—*Jonathan Swift*

Whiskey doesn't sustain life, but, whin taken hot with wather, a lump iv sugar, a piece iv lemon peel, and just th' dustin' iv the nutmeg-grater, it makes life sustainable.

—*Finley Peter Dunne*

He that drinks fast, pays slow.

—*Ben Franklin*

I exercise extreme self-control.

I never drink anything stronger than gin before breakfast.

—*W. C. Fields*

Licker talks mighty loud w'en it git loose fum de jug.

—*Joel Chandler Harris*

Any writer who wants to do his best against a deadline should stick to Coca-Cola.

—*John Kenneth Galbraith*

When pouring martinis, make sure they are filled dangerously close to the brim.

—*Joe McGuirk, bartender*

The saloon is the poor man's club.

—*Bishop Charles D. Williams*

Beer makes you smarter. It made Bud wiser.

—*Bill Mather*

There are two things that will be believed of any man whatsoever, and one of them is that he has taken to drink.

—*Booth Tarkington*

The prohibition law, written for weaklings and derelicts, has divided the nation, like Gaul, into three parts—wets, drys, and hypocrites.

—*Florence Sabin*

For a bad hangover, take the juice of two quarts of whiskey.

—*Eddie Condon*

Melancholy, indeed, should be diverted by every means but drinking.

—*Samuel Johnson*

Bad men live that they may eat and drink, whereas good men eat and drink that they may live.

—*Socrates*

But I'm not so think as you drunk I am.

—*Sir John Collings Squire*

There was that brief bout of how-could-we-have-been-so-cavalier-while-others-went-hungry-and-sick stoicism in the early 90's. Well evidently that's over with. Time to exhume those little black dresses and the point d'esprit. Long live the three-martini dinner! Cocktails are back. Tray chic.

—*Hal Rubenstein*

Drink not the third glass—which thou canst not tame when once it is within thee.

—*George Herbert*

I always keep a stimulant handy in case I see a snake—which I also keep handy.

—*W. C. Fields*

Let us eat and drink; for tomorrow we shall die.

—*Isaiah 22:13*

Questioner: If you had your life to live over, what would you do differently?

W.C. Fields: I'd live over a saloon.

Let him who sins when drunk, be punished when sober.

—*anonymous*

Either you're drunk or your braces are lopsided.

—*W. C. Fields*

I am sparkling; you are unusually talkative; he is drunk.

—New Statesman

When things get too unpleasant, I burn the day's newspaper, pull down the curtains, get out the jugs, and put in a civilized evening.

—H. L. Mencken

There is in all men a demand for the super-lative, so much so that the poor devil who has no other way of reaching it attains it by getting drunk.

—Oliver Wendell Holmes

Temperance is the control of all the functions of our bodies. The man who refuses liquor, goes in for apple pie and develops a paunch, is no ethical leader for me.

—*John Erskine*

I tried not drinking once. I heard myself talking all night and then, worse than that, next day I had total recall. It was terrifying.

—*Patsy (Joanna Lumley), in "Absolutely Fabulous"*

I have made an important discovery . . . that alcohol, taken in sufficient quantities, produces all the effects of intoxication.

—*Oscar Wilde*

Nothing ever tasted any better than a cold beer on a beautiful afternoon with nothing to look forward to but more of the same.

—*Hugh Hood*

Abstinence is as easy for me as temperance would be difficult.

—*Samuel Johnson*

Cocktails are in our blood. I myself come from a long line of martinis.

—*Glenn O'Brien*

When you look at the world through the bottom of a glass, may you see someone ready to buy.

—*Irish proverb*

A man hath no better thing under the sun, than to eat, and to drink, and to be merry.

—*Ecclesiastes 8:15*

So who's in a hurry?

—*Robert Benchley, on being warned that drinking is a*
slow death

We had gone out there to pass the beautiful
day of high summer like true Irishmen—locked
in the dark snug of a public house.

—*Brendan Behan*

The whole world is about three drinks behind.

—*Humphrey Bogart*

What do you want? Champagne?

Yes. Anything that will blur reality.

—*Patsy (Joanna Lumley) and Edina (Jennifer Saunders),
in "Absolutely Fabulous"*

Your ice is not cold enough.

—*Fiorello (Chico Marx), in* A Night at the Opera

How do you look when I'm sober?

—*Ring Lardner, to a stranger*

We frequently hear of people dying from too much drinking. That this happens is a matter of record. But the blame almost always is placed on whisky. Why this should be I never could understand. You can die from drinking too much of anything—coffee, water, milk, soft drinks and all such stuff as that. And so long as the presence of death lurks with anyone who goes through the simple act of swallowing, I will make mine whisky.

—W. C. Fields

In a tavern everybody puts on airs except the landlord.

—*Ralph Waldo Emerson*

The dipsomaniac and the abstainer are not only both mistaken, but they both make the same mistake. They both regard wine as a drug and not as a drink.

—*G. K. Chesterton*

When I drink, I think: and when I think, I drink.

—*François Rabelais*

Drinking is the soldier's pleasure.... Sweet is pleasure after pain.

—*John Dryden*

Frenchmen drink wine just like we used to drink water before Prohibition.

—Ring Lardner

Alcohol removes inhibitions—like that scared little mouse who got drunk and shook his whiskers and shouted: "Now bring on that damn cat!"

—Eleanor Early

Anybody who hates dogs and loves whiskey can't be all bad.

—W. C. Fields

A prohibitionist is the sort of man one wouldn't care to drink with—even if he drank.

—*H. L. Mencken*

And Noah he often said to his wife when he sat down to dine,

"I don't care where the water goes if it doesn't get into the wine."

—*G. K. Chesterton*

The rat stops gnawing the wood, the dungeon walls withdraw, the weight is lifted...your pulse steadies and the sun has found your heart, the day was not bad, the season has not been bad, there is sense and even promise in going on.

   —*Bernard De Voto, in praise of the martini*

Alcohol was the background color in the fabric of Reggie's life.

   —*Barbara Goldsmith, on Gloria Vanderbilt's father*

Well, all right, but it is cold on the stomach.

—*Joseph Stalin, on accepting a martini mixed by*
Franklin D. Roosevelt

If I displayed this cup, I might look at it once or twice a week. By using it, I get pleasure from it continually.

—*Lila Acheson Wallace, on sipping a martini from a*
four-thousand-year-old Egyptian cup

This is an excellent martini—sort of tastes like it isn't there at all, just a cold cloud.

—*Herman Wouk*

Russians will consume marinated mushrooms and vodka, salted herring and vodka, smoked salmon and vodka, salami and vodka, caviar on brown bread and vodka, pickled cucumbers and vodka, cold tongue and vodka, red beet salad and vodka, scallions and vodka—anything and everything and vodka.

—*Hedrick Smith*

I am prepared to believe that a dry martini slightly impairs the palate, but think what it does for the soul.

—*Alec Waugh*

I decided to stop drinking with creeps.
I decided to drink only with friends.
I've lost 30 pounds.

—*Ernest Hemingway*

The condition of inebriation is very nearly a universal experience and the words come from all our societal venues—the fraternity house, debutante ball, literary luncheon, longshoreman's bar, the Wild West.

—*Bruce Weber*

Some writers take to drink, others take to audiences.

—*Gore Vidal*

That genuine extract from a wine journal is the sort of thing that gets the stuff a bad name with a lot of people who would enjoy wine if they could face trying it seriously....

—*Kingsley Amis*

Have ready a bottle of brandy, because I always feel like drinking that heroic drink when we talk ontological heroics together.

—*Herman Melville, to Nathaniel Hawthorne*

He has a profound respect for old age. Especially when it's bottled.

—*Gene Fowler, on W. C. Fields's fondness for*

aged bourbon

It is better to have bread left over than to run short of wine.

—*Spanish proverb*

Wonderful, varied words. Blitzed, blasted, blotto, bombed, cockeyed, crocked, ripped, looped, loaded, leveled, wasted, wiped, soused, sozzled, smashed, and schnockered. Stewed, stinko, stupid, tanked, totaled, tight, and tipsy. Not to mention feeling no pain, three sheets to the wind, in one's cups, intoxicated, addle-pated, and pixilated.

—*Bruce Weber*

Try substituting the word "women" for the word "drinking" in the AA questionnaire. Are women affecting your peace of mind? Are women making your home life unhappy? Do you show a marked moodiness since women? Are women disturbing the harmony of your life? Have women changed your personality? Do you crave a woman at a definite time daily? Do you require a woman next morning? Do you prefer a woman alone? Have women made you irritable? Yes, yes, yes, and again yes.

—*Jeffrey Bernard*

This physical loathing for alcohol I have never got over. But I have conquered it. To this day I conquer it every time I take a drink.

—*Jack London*

Italian wine was something rough and red that came in a straw-covered flask.... With a candle stuck in its neck, the empty bottle was an unmistakable badge of sophomore sophistication.

—*Nancy Harmon Jenkins*

I'm very fond of alcohol, but I drink a minute amount compared with what I did at one period in my life, when I drank at least a bottle of brandy a night plus gins and things during the day. Now I'll have a dry sherry around noon, maybe a glass of wine at lunch and then in the evening I'll have two or three gin and tonics and half a bottle of wine and probably a couple of brandies, which for me is practically being teetotal.

—*George Melly*

Whenever someone asks me if I want water with my Scotch, I say I'm thirsty, not dirty.

—*Joe E. Lewis*

The men were so busy looking at the women, they didn't drink.

—*Hank Leslie, on the day that the Biltmore Hotel's Men's Bar first admitted women*

You can't be a true bleacher creature drinking this kind of beer.

—*Stan Johnson, on low-calorie beer's being sold at the Detroit Tigers stadium*

No thanks, I don't drink.

—Jeff Stone, major league outfielder, on being asked if
he would like a shrimp cocktail before dinner

Short-term amnesia is not the worst affliction if you have an Irish flair for the sauce.

—Norman Mailer

The relationship between a Russian and a bottle of vodka is almost mystical.

—Richard Owen, on Soviet efforts to decrease drinking

More than a pint, less than a quart.

—*Ann L. Maytag, appliance heiress, when asked about*
her daily drinking habits

When the rich man falls down it is an accident; when a poor man falls, he is called drunk.

—*Turkish proverb*

When you stop drinking, you have to deal with this marvelous personality that started you drinking in the first place.

—*Jimmy Breslin*

A good heavy book holds you down. It's an anchor that keeps you from getting up and having another gin and tonic.

—*Roy Blount Jr.*

If four or five guys tell you that you're drunk, even though you know you haven't had a thing to drink, the least you can do is to lie down a little while.

—*Joseph Schenck*

The three-martini lunch is the epitome of American efficiency. Where else can you get an earful, a bellyful and a snootful at the same time?

—*Gerald R. Ford*

I know folks all have a tizzy about it, but I like a little bourbon of an evening. It helps me sleep. I don't much care what they say about it.

—*Lillian Carter, mother of President Jimmy Carter*

He resolved, having done it once, never to move his eyeballs again.

—*Kingsley Amis, on recovering from a hangover*

The Americans are a funny lot: they drink whiskey to keep them warm; then they put some ice in it to make it cool; they put some sugar in it to make it sweet, and then they put a slice of lemon in it to make it sour. Then they say "here's to you" and drink it themselves.

—B. N. Chakravarty

The drink is slipping its little hand into yours.

—J. Bryan. III, on the start of a perfect weekend

Well, between Scotch and nothin', I suppose I'd take Scotch. It's the nearest thing to good moonshine I can find.

—*William Faulkner*

New York is the greatest city in the world for lunch. . . . And when that first martini hits the liver like a silver bullet, there is a sigh of contentment that can be heard in Dubuque.

—*William Emerson Jr.*

Beer has long been the prime lubricant in our social intercourse and the sacred throat-anointing fluid that accompanies the ritual of mateship. To sink a few cold ones with the blokes is both an escape and a confirmation of belonging.

—*Rennie Ellis, on beer drinking in Australia*

No, Sir; there is nothing which has yet been contrived by man, by which so much happiness is produced as by a good tavern or inn.

—*James Boswell*

When evening quickens in the street, comes a pause in the day's occupation that is known as the cocktail hour. It marks the lifeward turn. The heart wakens from coma and its dyspnea ends . . . to believe that the world has not been altogether lost or, if lost, then not altogether in vain.

—*Bernard De Voto*

My final warning to you is always pay for your own drinks. . . . All the scandals in the world of politics today have their cause in the despicable habit of swallowing free drinks.

—Y. Yakigawa, president, Kyoto University, advising students

ABOUT THE AUTHOR

Jess Brallier is a publisher, author, and web publisher. He has authored or co-authored more than thirty books, including both adult's and children's titles. In 1995, Brallier founded the children's publishing imprint, Planet Dexter. He has won book publishing's LMP Individual Achievement Award in recognition of his marketing campaigns for three *New York Times* bestsellers. A native of Ligonier, Pennsylvania, Brallier is a graduate of the University of Pittsburgh and Boston University. He resides in West Hollywood, California, with his wife.

JESS BRALLIER

FROM OPEN ROAD MEDIA

OPEN ROAD
INTEGRATED MEDIA

OPEN ROAD

INTEGRATED MEDIA

Find a full list of our authors and
titles at www.openroadmedia.com

FOLLOW US
@OpenRoadMedia